Year 3
Book 2

Acknowledgements

Author Team:
Val Pilkington-Smith
Belinda Evans
Adam Higgins
Lisa Morris
Laura Nolan
Sue Thorn
Rebecca Harman

Specialist Team Coordinator:
Jill Clare

Specialist Maths Consultant:
Barbara Allebone

© 2002 Folens Limited, on behalf of the authors.

United Kingdom: Folens Publishers, Apex Business Centre, Boscombe Road, Dunstable, LU5 4RL.
Email: folens@folens.com

Ireland: Folens Publishers, Greenhills Road, Tallaght, Dublin 24.
Email: info@folens.ie

Poland: JUKA, ul. Renesansowa 38, Warsaw 01-905.

Folens publications are protected by international copyright laws. All rights are reserved. The copyright of all materials in this publication, except where otherwise stated, remains the property of the publisher and authors. No part of this publication may be reproduced, stored in a retrieval system, or transmitted, in any form or by any means, for whatever purpose, without the written permission of Folens Limited.

Val Pilkington-Smith, Belinda Evans, Adam Higgins, Lisa Morris, Laura Nolan, Sue Thorn and Rebecca Harman hereby assert their moral rights to be identified as the authors of this work in accordance with the Copyright, Designs and Patents Act 1988.

Editors: Mark Haslam and June Hall
Layout artist: Suzanne Ward
Cover design: Duncan McTeer
Illustrations: Chantal Kees

This edition first published 2002 by Folens Limited. Based on the Folens Maths Programme (Teacher Files) published 1999–2000.

Every effort has been made to trace the copyright holders of material used in this publication. If any copyright holder has been overlooked, we should be pleased to make any necessary arrangements.

British Library Cataloguing in Publication Data. A catalogue record for this publication is available from the British Library.

ISBN 1 84303 196-5

Contents

Puzzle pieces	1
Making numbers	2
Three in a row	3
Routes to 10 and 20	4
Combinations to 10	5
Near doubles	6
Number patterns	7
Banker	8
Pounds and pence	9
Shopkeeper	10
Boxes	11
Battleships	12
Which direction?	13
Space mission	14
Shape grid	15
It's a date	16
How old?	17
Make your own	18
Heavier or lighter than 1kg?	19
How heavy?	20
Adders and ladders	21
Add 15, add 25	22
Patterns and sequences	23
TU addition	24
How many steps?	25
Add or subtract?	26
Checking calculations	27
How many ways?	28
Tables	29

Contents

Digit shift	30
Division pairs	31
Remainder game	32
Four squares	33
How many fifths in a whole?	34
Colour fractions	35
Fraction wall	36
Ordering fractions	37
Sweet bar charts	38
Colourful cubes	39
Bird study	40
Carroll clowns	41
Venn clowns	42

Puzzle pieces

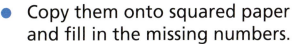

You will need: squared paper

★ Work with a partner.

- Below are some pieces from a hundred square.
- Copy them onto squared paper and fill in the missing numbers.
- Discuss the missing numbers with your partner before you fill them in.

①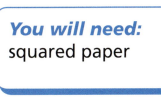

④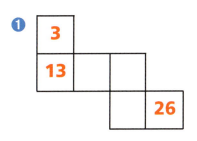

②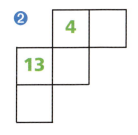

③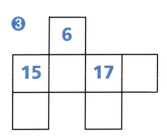

⑤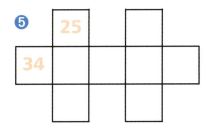

⑥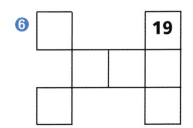

⑦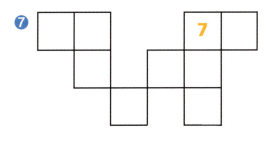

⑧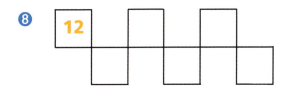

⑨ What does moving one place to the right on a hundred square add to a number?

⑩ What does moving one place down on a hundred square add to a number?

 I can work out numbers 1 or 10 more or less than a given number.

Week 1 Lesson 1

Making numbers

★ How many three-digit numbers can you make from the following digits? Record all the numbers you think of.

① 3, 7 and 2

273

② 8, 5 and 9

③ 1, 6 and 7

176

④ 4, 9 and 3

⑤ 6, 2 and 5

652

⑥ 4, 7 and 7

⑦ 8, 3 and 3

833

8635

★ What happens when two of the digits are the same?

★ How many four-digit numbers can you make from the digits 6, 3, 8 and 5?

Write out all the numbers you have thought of in order of size, starting with the smallest.

Try to think of a way you can make sure that you do not miss any numbers out.

I can write and order numbers.

Three in a row

You will need:
two sets of number cards 0–9
counters

★ Work with a partner.
★ Take turns to turn over two cards and make a two-digit number.
★ Round the number to the nearest 10 and cover that multiple of 10 with a counter.
★ If the space is already covered you may replace the counter with your own.
★ Shuffle the cards after each turn.
★ The first player with three in a row wins.

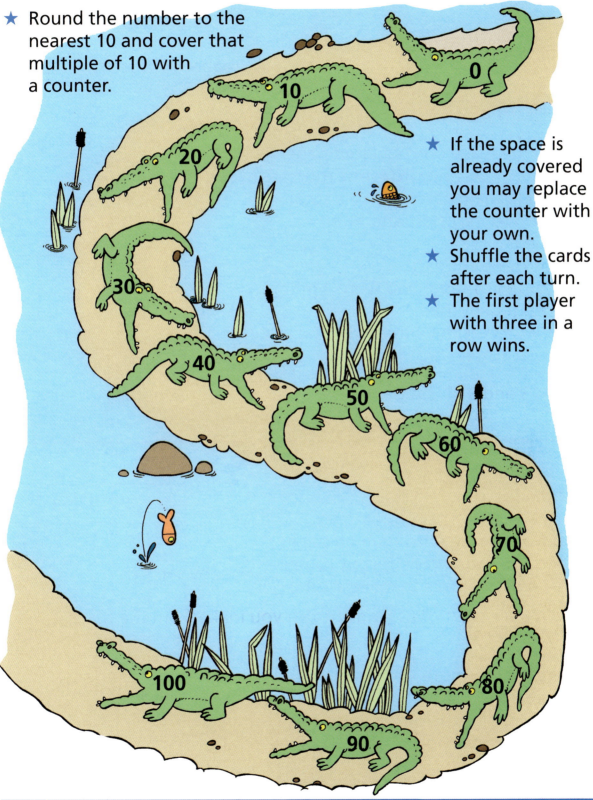

Week 1 Lesson 3

I can round two-digit numbers to the nearest 10.

Routes to 10 and 20

You will need:
squared paper
two different coloured pencils

★ Work with a partner. You should each use a different coloured pencil.

The more digits you use, the higher your score.

❶ Make 10

- Copy the maze onto squared paper. Take turns to find **different** routes through the maze to make a total of 10. You may start and finish anywhere.
- Have five turns each.
- Record each route and score 1 point for each digit used.
- The winner is the player with the highest score.

4	2	4	2	1
1	3	2	7	0
2	1	1	3	8
3	1	1	5	1
9	2	6	1	3

Example
9 + 1 = 10
(2 points)

❷ Make 20

- Copy the maze onto squared paper.
- Take turns to find **different** routes through the maze to make a total of 20. You may start and finish anywhere.
- Have five turns each.
- Record each route and score 1 point for each digit used.
- The winner is the player with the highest score.

1	4	9	8	3
7	8	2	7	12
3	10	2	5	1
1	11	6	1	4
4	3	7	3	9

Example
9 + 4 + 1 + 6 = 20
(4 points)

 I can combine numbers to make 10 and 20.

Combinations to 10

You will need:
two sets of number cards 0–9
a timer

★ Work with a partner.

❶ Write down as many combinations of three numbers that total 10 as you can in five minutes.

For example: 2 + 5 + 3 = 10

Compare your answers with your partner.

❷ Turn over five number cards and add them together. Look for combinations to help you add them together, for example:

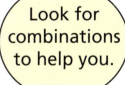
Look for combinations to help you.

| 2 | 6 | 3 | 4 | 1 |

6 + 4 = 10

10 + 2 + 3 + 1 = 16
or 2 + 3 + 4 + 1 = 10   10 + 6 = 16

 5   5

Record the methods you use and discuss other strategies with your partner.

Challenge

★ Add up all the number cards.

I can use number bonds in addition.

Week 2 Lesson 2

Near doubles

★ Use your knowledge of doubles to solve the following questions. Show your method, for example:

> 5 + 6 =   double 5 is 10   10 + 1 = 11

❶ 10 + 11 =

❷ 12 + 13 =

❸ 16 + 15 =

❹ 20 + 22 =

❺ 27 + 25 =

❻ 98 + 99 =

★ Now work out the scores on these dartboards. (The inner ring scores double.)

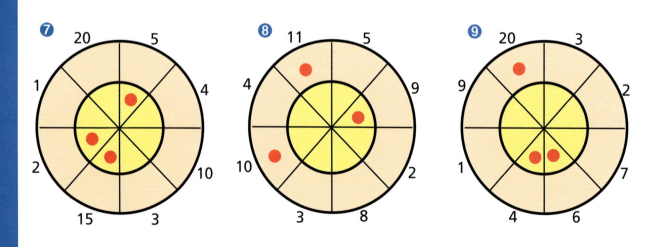

Challenge

★ Can you score 50 on each dartboard using three darts?
★ Try other totals.

I can use doubles and near doubles for addition.

Number patterns

★ Look for patterns to solve the following questions.

① 4 + 9 = 13
4 + 19 = 23
4 + 29 = ☐

② 5 + 5 = 10
5 + 25 = 30
5 + 45 = ☐

③ 14 + 12 = 26
☐ + 12 = 36
34 + 12 = ☐

④ 9 + 15 = 24
29 + 15 = ☐
☐ + 15 = 64

⑤ 38 + 9 = 47
28 + 9 = ☐
18 + ☐ = 27
☐ + 9 = 17

⑥ 78 + 16 = 94
58 + ☐ = 74
☐ + 16 = 54
18 + 16 = ☐

⑦ 93 + ☐ = 99
☐ + 6 = 69
33 + 6 = ☐

⑧ 125 + ☐ = 150
100 + 25 = 125
☐ + 25 = 100

Think carefully.

⑨ 34 + 11 = 45
34 + 22 = ☐
34 + 33 = ☐

⑩ 80 + 15 = 95
80 + 30 = ☐
80 + 45 = ☐

★ I can use patterns in calculations to solve problems.

Banker

You will need:
banking cards
counters
a dice
selection of coins totalling £3 for each player and the bank

★ Work with a partner.
★ Place the cards face down in a pile.
★ Take turns to throw the dice.
★ If you land on a star, pick a card. You will either spend some of your money or receive some from the bank.
★ If you land on a square you can exchange some of your coins for **one** coin of an equivalent value from the bank.
★ The aim is to get rid of as many of your coins as possible.
★ The winner is the player with the least number of coins at the end of the game.

 I can exchange small value coins for a larger value coin.

Pounds and pence

You will need:
number cards 0–20

★ Copy this table into your book.

Pounds	Pence	Decimals

★ Turn over a card. Write the number in the 'pounds' column.
★ Turn over another card. Write the number in the 'pence' column.
★ Then write the number using decimals.

Example:

Pounds	Pence	Decimals
4	18	£4.18
1	2	£1.02

★ Repeat this exercise nine more times.

I can use decimal notation for money.

Shopkeeper

You will need:
number lines
selection of coins
paper clip

★ Work in groups of three or four.
★ One player is a shopkeeper with a float of change.
★ The other players are customers each with the following coins to spend:

★ The customers take turns to spin a paper clip around the point of a pencil on the grid below.
They must select the right coins for the amount shown and give them to the shopkeeper. You can use a number line to help you.

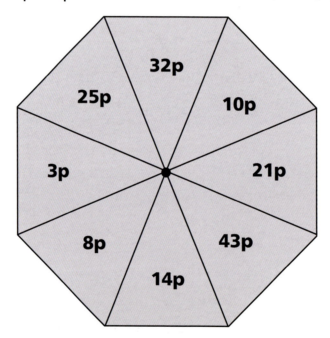

★ The shopkeeper must select the right coins to give as change and count it into the customer's hand.
★ The customers should keep a record of their 'purchases'. If they do not have enough money to buy an item they miss that turn.
★ The winner is the one who spends most of their money after five turns each.

I can make totals and give change.

Boxes

You will need:
two dice (one labelled 1–6 and one labelled A–F)
two colouring pencils
squared paper

★ Work with a partner.

Game 1

★ Copy this grid onto squared paper.

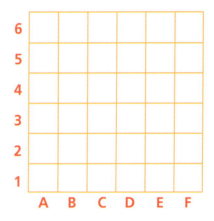

★ Take turns to throw both dice.
★ Find the square that corresponds to the dice and colour it in (in your chosen colour).
★ If the square is already coloured in, miss a turn.
★ The winner is the first player to make a box of four squares, like this:

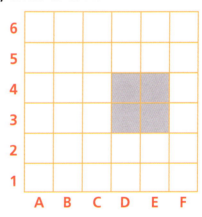

Game 2

★ Make another copy of the grid above on to squared paper.
★ Repeat the game as above, but change the rules to one of the following:
  • The winner is the first to colour in three squares in a row.
  • The winner is the first to colour in four squares in a row.
  • The winner is the player with most squares coloured in when the grid is full.

 I can find positions on a grid.

Battleships

You will need: squared paper

★ Work with a partner.
★ Each copy the grid below onto squared paper.

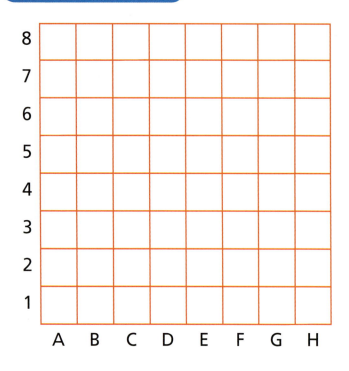

★ On your grid, plot the following five ships:

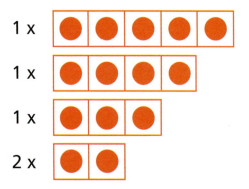

★ The ships must not touch each other.
★ Do not let your partner see your grid.
★ Take turns to guess the location of your partner's ships.
★ Make another copy each of the grid and record your guesses on it (x = miss, o = hit).
★ The winner is the first player to locate all of their partner's battleships.

 I can plot positions on a grid.

Which direction?

You will need: squared paper

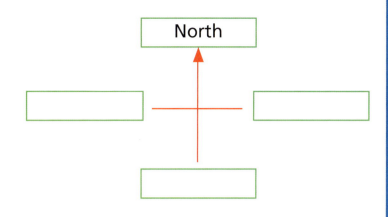

❶ Copy and complete these compass points.

Work with a partner.

❷ You are going to describe a route to your partner using compass directions.

Example:

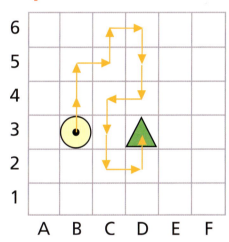

Start B3 →N →N →E →N →
E →S →S →W →S →
S →E →N End D3

★ Copy this grid twice onto squared paper.

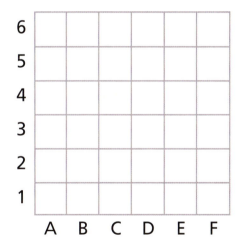

★ Take turns to draw a route and describe it to your partner.
★ When you finish you should both have the same pattern.
★ Have two turns each.

I can use compass points to give directions.

Week 4 Lesson 3

Space mission

You will need: squared paper

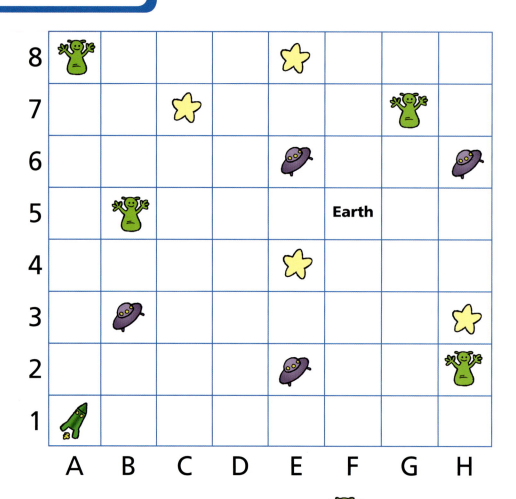

1. Write down the positions of the aliens.

2. Write down the positions of the stars.

3. Write down the positions of the spaceships.

4. Guide the rocket back to Earth using only the empty squares. Describe the quickest route using N, S, E and W.

Challenge

★ Draw your own grid like the one above on squared paper. It could be a treasure island, a park, a beach or anything you want. Write some questions for another pupil to answer.

I can name positions on a grid using the compass points.

Shape grid

You will need: shape cards

★ Work in groups of three or four.
★ Each draw a grid like the one below onto a sheet of paper. Each square must be 5cm x 5cm.

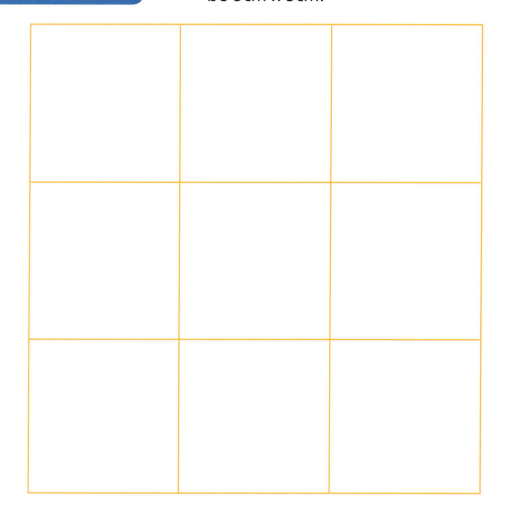

★ Take turns to choose a shape card and place it on your grid (do not let the other members of your group see your grid).
★ Describe your shape (do not name it) and its position on your grid.

Example:
Put the shape with six sides of the same length in the centre square.

★ The other players must put that shape in the same position on their grids.
★ When all the positions are full, show each other your grids.
★ You should all have the same pattern of shapes.

Useful words: above, below, right, left, up, down, north, south, east, west, sides, corners, curves, vertex, edge, symmetrical.

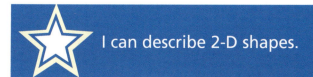

I can describe 2-D shapes.

Week 4 Lesson 5

It's a date

Use the calendars on **RS** 'Calendars' to help you answer these questions.

On what day is:

1. 6 July?
2. 23 July?
3. 15 November?
4. 19 November?
5. 30 June?
6. 1 December?
7. Christmas day (25 December)?
8. How many Wednesdays are there in July?
9. How many Mondays are there in November?
10. Are there the same number of Mondays in November every year?

Challenge

★ Complete a calendar for the current month. Use today's date as a starting point.
★ Write some questions for a friend to answer.

I can use a calendar.

How old?

★ Work in groups of three or four.

❶ A child is 300 days old. What is their age in weeks?
Discuss how you will work this out and how you will record your method.

> **Examples:**
>
> - There are seven days in one week
>   14 days in two weeks
>   28 days in four weeks.
>
> - There are seven days in one week
>   70 days in 10 weeks
>   140 days in 20 weeks.

★ Work on your own.

❷ A child was born 2000 days ago. What is their age:

  a. in weeks?

  b. in months?

  c. in years?

I can work with different units

Week 5 Lesson 2

Make your own

★ Work in groups of three or four.

★ You are going to make a set of 'chase the answer' cards for another group to use.

- Draw 16 boxes on a sheet of paper.
- You need to write a time and an instruction in each box.
- Each instruction must lead to the time in the next box.

Examples:

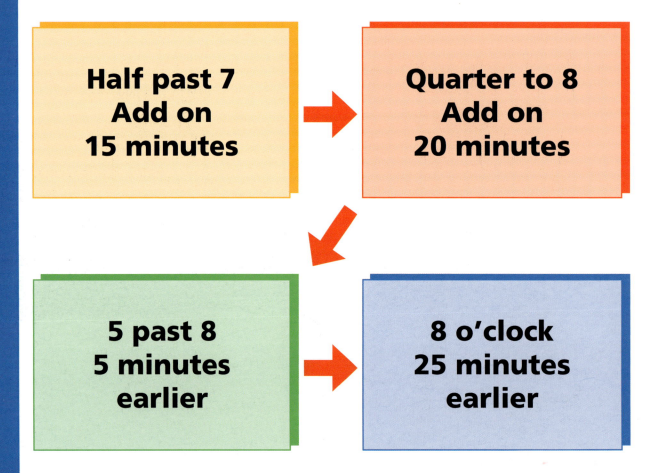

- Continue until you have filled in your 16 boxes.
- The instruction in the last box must lead back to the time in the first box.
- Give your 'chase the answer' cards to another group to read out loud.

Heavier or lighter than 1kg?

You will need:
a 1kg weight
balancing scales
a variety of objects to weigh

★ Hold a 1kg weight in one hand and an object (for example a book) in the other.

★ Estimate whether the object is heavier or lighter than 1kg.

★ Record your estimate on a copy of the table below:

Object	Estimate	Check
reading book	lighter	lighter ✓

★ Check your estimate using balancing scales.

 I can compare the mass of objects.

How heavy?

  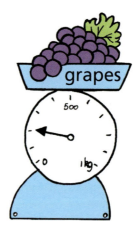 

❶ Which fruit weighs most?

❷ Which fruit weighs least?

❸ How much lighter than the pears are the apples?

❹ Which fruit weighs exactly half as much as the pears?

 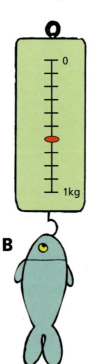 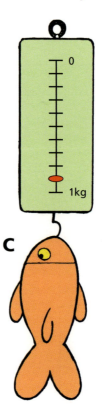 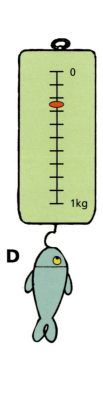

A   B   C   D

❺ Which fish is heaviest?

❻ Which fish is lightest?

❼ How much heavier is fish C than fish D?

 I can read scales divided into 100g.

Adders and ladders

You will need:
two dice
counters

★ Work in groups of three or four.

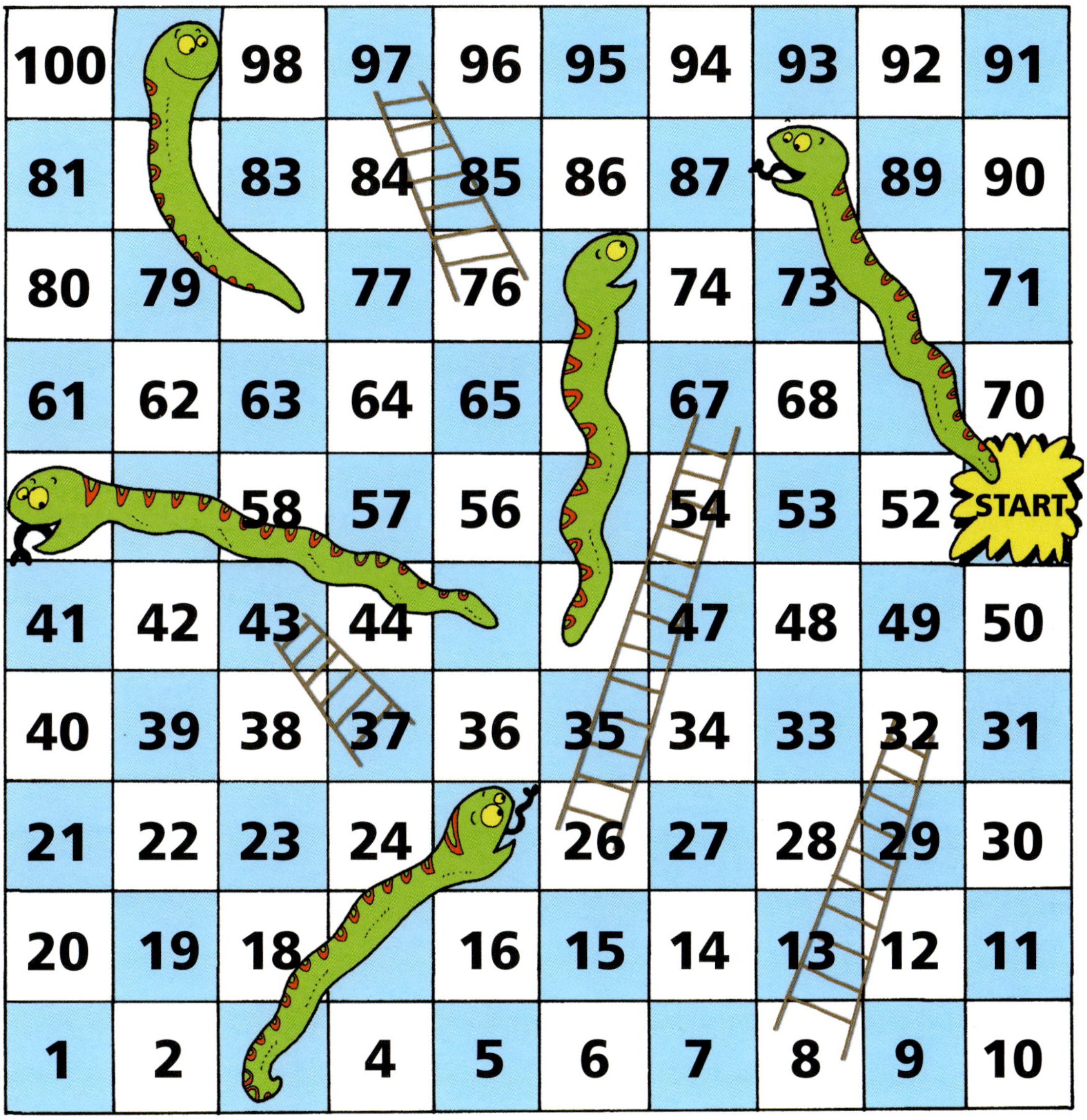

Week 8 Lessons 1, 2 and 3

Rules

★ Place your counter on 'Start'.
★ Take turns to throw both dice.
★ Move forwards (+) or backwards (−) the given number of squares.
★ Go up a ladder if you land at the bottom of one, and down a snake if you land on its mouth.
★ The winner is the player who reaches 100 first.

Add 15, add 25

> **You will need:**
> number lines

Add 15

★ You are going to look at how to add 15 to a number.
★ You can split 15 into three single 'jumps' on a number line.

Example:

27 + 15

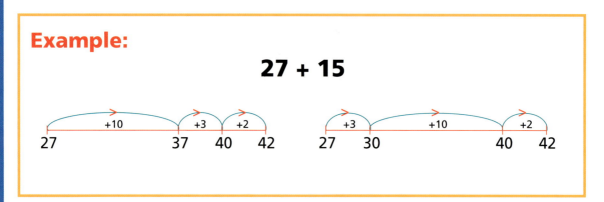

★ Answer the following questions, using the number line to help you.

1. 12 + 15 =
2. 22 + 15 =
3. 37 + 15 =
4. 52 + 15 =
5. 77 + 15 =

Add 25

★ Now work out how you would add 25 to the following numbers. Use the number line to help you.

6. 17 + 25 =
7. 27 + 25 =
8. 32 + 25 =
9. 62 + 25 =
10. 87 + 25 =

I can add numbers in different ways using number lines.

Patterns and sequences

★ Copy and complete each pattern below and explain the rule.

① 0, 2, 4, 6, ☐, ☐

② 50, 45, 40, 35, ☐, ☐

③ 22, 32, 42, 52, ☐, ☐

④ 601, 501, 401, ☐, ☐

⑤ 41, 36, 31, 26, ☐, ☐

⑥ 98, 96, 94, 92, ☐, ☐

⑦ 12, 17, 22, 27, ☐, ☐

⑧ Here is a pattern of sticks. Draw shapes **d** and **e** in the same sequence.

a. ☐   b. ☐   c. ☐

Copy and complete the table.

Shape	a	b	c	d	e
Sticks	4	8			

I can complete and explain patterns.

TU addition

You will need:
number lines

★ You are going to look at different ways of adding up numbers.

> **Example:**
>
> 24 + 13 + 22
>
> Separate each number into tens and units:
>
> 20 and 4   10 and 3   20 and 2
>
> These can be added together in different ways, but the answer is always the same:
>
> 20 + 10 + 20 = 50
> 4 + 3 + 2 = 9
> 50 + 9 = 59
>
> 20 + 4 + 3 + 2 = 29
> 10 + 20 = 30
> 29 + 30 = 59

Now try to find different ways of adding the following numbers. You can use a number line to help you.

1. 11 + 25 + 12

2. 32 + 31 + 33

3. 25 + 13 + 41

4. 12 + 23 + 26

5. 35 + 46 + 22

I can add numbers in different ways.

How many steps?

You will need:
two packs of number cards 0–9
number lines

Week 9 Lesson 2

★ Work in groups of three or four.

- Take turns to turn over four cards and make 2 two-digit numbers.

- All members of the group should subtract the smaller number from the larger number.

Example:

7 6 − 4 1 = 35

- Write down your method on a number line.

- Explain your method to the rest of the group and compare the number of steps each of you made.

- Continue the exercise until all members of the group have had three turns each.

I can subtract two-digit numbers using a number line.

Add or subtract?

> **You will need:**
> two counters with + on one side and – on the other

★ Throw both counters.
★ Write a 'real-life' problem involving the operations shown on your counters.

Example:

You throw a + and a –.

There are 32 passengers on a bus. 12 get on at the first stop and 15 get off at the next stop. How many passengers are still on the bus?

★ Repeat the exercise five more times.
★ Swap your questions with a classmate and solve each other's problems.

The answer to the above problem would be:
32 + 12 = 44
44 – 15 = 29

I can write and solve 'real-life' problems.

Checking calculations

★ Solve the problems below.
★ When you have solved each one, check it using a different method or the inverse.

> **Example:**
>
> | | Method 1 | A different method |
> |---|---|---|
> | 45 + 46 | 40 + 40 = 80 | 45 + 45 = 80 + 10 |
> | | 5 + 6 = 11 | 80 + 10 + 1 = 91 |
> | | 80 + 11 = 91 | |

❶ 27 + 36 + 19   Use a different method to check your answer.

❷ 125 + 248   Use a different method to check your answer.

❸ 101 − 85   Use a different method to check your answer.

❹ 36 + 94   Use the inverse to check your answer.

❺ 110 − 30   Use the inverse to check your answer.

I can check my calculations using a different method or the inverse operation.

Week 9 Lesson 5

How many ways?

You will need: number cards 1–50

★ Work in groups of three or four.

- Take turns to pick a card and record the number shown.
- Next to this number write down all the ways you can use multiplication facts to make this number.
- Record the number of ways you can make the number and score one point for each.
- Have five turns each.
- The winner is the player with the most points.

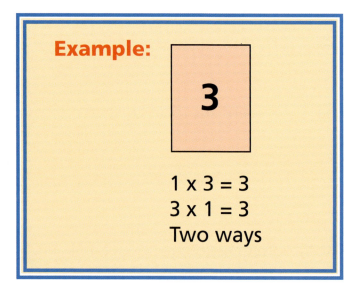

Example:

3

1 x 3 = 3
3 x 1 = 3
Two ways

- You can use the multiplication tables on the next page to help you.
- Can any numbers be made an odd number of ways?
- Are there any numbers that cannot be made?

I can multiply in any order.

Tables

x1

1 x 1 = 1
2 x 1 = 2
3 x 1 = 3
4 x 1 = 4
5 x 1 = 5
6 x 1 = 6
7 x 1 = 7
8 x 1 = 8
9 x 1 = 9
10 x 1 = 10

x2

1 x 2 = 2
2 x 2 = 4
3 x 2 = 6
4 x 2 = 8
5 x 2 = 10
6 x 2 = 12
7 x 2 = 14
8 x 2 = 16
9 x 2 = 18
10 x 2 = 20

x3

1 x 3 = 3
2 x 3 = 6
3 x 3 = 9
4 x 3 = 12
5 x 3 = 15
6 x 3 = 18
7 x 3 = 21
8 x 3 = 24
9 x 3 = 27
10 x 3 = 30

x4

1 x 4 = 4
2 x 4 = 8
3 x 4 = 12
4 x 4 = 16
5 x 4 = 20
6 x 4 = 24
7 x 4 = 28
8 x 4 = 32
9 x 4 = 36
10 x 4 = 40

x5

1 x 5 = 5
2 x 5 = 10
3 x 5 = 15
4 x 5 = 20
5 x 5 = 25
6 x 5 = 30
7 x 5 = 35
8 x 5 = 40
9 x 5 = 45
10 x 5 = 50

x6

1 x 6 = 6
2 x 6 = 12
3 x 6 = 18
4 x 6 = 24
5 x 6 = 30
6 x 6 = 36
7 x 6 = 42
8 x 6 = 48
9 x 6 = 54
10 x 6 = 60

x7

1 x 7 = 7
2 x 7 = 14
3 x 7 = 21
4 x 7 = 28
5 x 7 = 35
6 x 7 = 42
7 x 7 = 49
8 x 7 = 56
9 x 7 = 63
10 x 7 = 70

x8

1 x 8 = 8
2 x 8 = 16
3 x 8 = 24
4 x 8 = 32
5 x 8 = 40
6 x 8 = 48
7 x 8 = 56
8 x 8 = 64
9 x 8 = 72
10 x 8 = 80

x9

1 x 9 = 9
2 x 9 = 18
3 x 9 = 27
4 x 9 = 36
5 x 9 = 45
6 x 9 = 54
7 x 9 = 63
8 x 9 = 72
9 x 9 = 81
10 x 9 = 90

x10

1 x 10 = 10
2 x 10 = 20
3 x 10 = 30
4 x 10 = 40
5 x 10 = 50
6 x 10 = 60
7 x 10 = 70
8 x 10 = 80
9 x 10 = 90
10 x 10 = 100

Week 10 Lesson 1

Digit shift

You will need:
number cards 0–9
cards marked x10 and x100

★ Work in groups of three or four.

- Place the number cards in one pile and the x10/x100 cards in another pile.
- Take turns to choose a card from each pile.
- Multiply the two numbers together and record your answer.
- You have six chances to get close to 1000 without going over.
- You can stick at any point in the game.
- Keep records of each turn.

Example:

3 x 10 = 30
4 x 100 = 400
1 x 100 = 100
9 x 10 = 90
3 x 100 = 300

Stick

Working:
400 + 100 = 500
90 + 30 = 120
500 + 120 = 620
620 + 300 = 920 (stick)

★ I can use knowledge of place value to add mentally.

Division pairs

★ You are going to practise division by grouping.

★ Find as many different ways as you can of dividing 20 into equal parts.

★ Record your division sentences.

Example:

20 ÷ 1 = 20

20 ÷ 2 = 10

20 ÷ 4 = 5

20 ÷ 5 = 4

20 ÷ 10 = 2

20 ÷ 20 = 1

★ Look for pairs of sentences that use the same numbers.

★ All of your sentences should belong to a pair.

Example:

20 ÷ 1 = 20 and 20 ÷ 20 = 1

20 ÷ 2 = 10 and 20 ÷ 10 = 2

20 ÷ 4 = 5 and 20 ÷ 5 = 4

★ Repeat the exercise for the following numbers: 12, 16 and 24.

I can divide by grouping.

Remainder game

You will need:
number cards 1–50
dice labelled 1, 2, 3, 4, 5, 10

★ Work in groups of three or four.
★ You are going to play a division game.

- Take turns to turn over a card and throw the dice.
- Make a division sentence, for example, the number on the card divided by the number on the dice.
- Write your division sentence down and work out the answer.
- Check that everyone in your group agrees that your answer is correct.
- Score 1 point for each remainder in your answer.

36 ÷ 10 = 3 remainder 6

Score 6 points

- Have six turns each.
- The winner is the player who scores the most points.

I can work out a division sentence that has a remainder.

Four squares

You will need:
counters

★ Work in groups of three or four.

• Take turns to choose a number on the grid below.

16	28	30	32	18	4
8	100	24	8	15	27
36	10	6	5	6	22
7	70	20	12	50	12
45	8	3	90	40	35
14	42	2	16	20	6

• Write a division sentence starting with that number.
• If you can write a second division sentence and two multiplication sentences to complete the family, cover the square with a counter (each player should use a different coloured counter).

Example:

6     $6 \div 3 = 2$ $3 \times 2 = 6$
      $6 \div 2 = 3$ $2 \times 3 = 6$

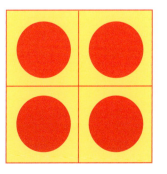

• The winner is the first player to cover a square of four numbers.

I can write families of multiplication and division statements.

Week 10 Lesson 5

How many fifths in a whole?

You will need:
squared paper

★ A pentomino is a shape made using five squares joined along their edges.

 ✓

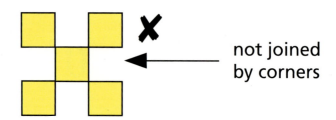 ✗ ← not joined by corners

★ How many different pentominoes can you draw on squared paper?

Remember:

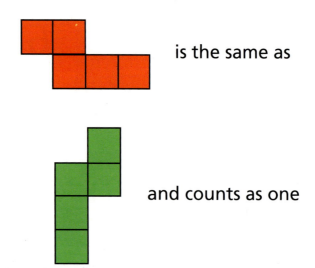

is the same as

and counts as one

★ Colour in each pentomino using a maximum of three colours (you may use just one or two). Next to each pentomino write what fraction you have coloured in each colour. Try not to use the same combination twice.

Example:

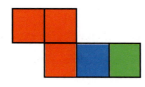

Red – $\frac{3}{5}$

Blue – $\frac{1}{5}$

Green – $\frac{1}{5}$

I can recognise fifths.

Colour fractions

> **You will need:**
> interlocking cubes in four different colours

★ Choose ten cubes in the following colours:
- one green
- two red
- two blue
- five yellow

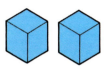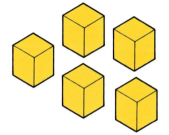

❶ Connect the cubes together as a rod.
What fraction of the rod is:
- green
- red
- blue
- yellow?

❷ Mix the ten cubes and put them together in a different order.
What fraction of the rod is:
- green
- red
- blue
- yellow?

❸ Make as many different rods as you can with different colour combinations using ten cubes. For each rod, record the fractions of each colour.

I can find fractions of shapes.

Fraction wall

You will need: equivalence dominoes

★ Work with a partner.

❶ Make a copy of the fraction wall below and fill in the spaces.

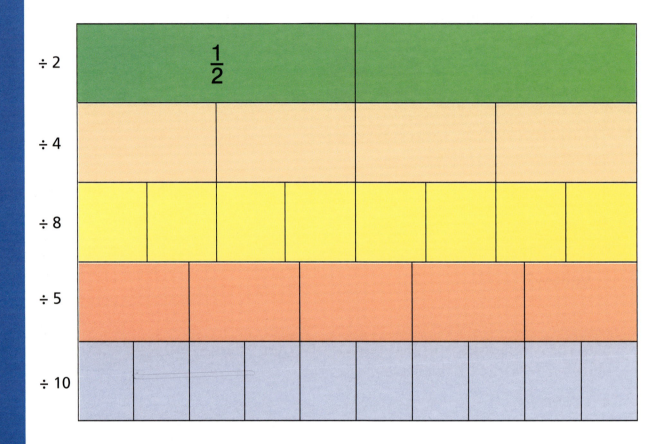

❷ Play dominoes with a set of equivalence dominoes.
Use your completed fraction wall to check matching dominoes.

I can recognise equivalent fractions.

Ordering fractions

You will need:
fraction cards

★ Work with a partner.

• Shuffle the fraction cards and place them face down in a pile.

• Take turns to choose two cards.

• Decide if you should put a > sign, a < sign or an = sign between them.

• Write your number sentence down, then put the cards to the bottom of the pack.

Example:

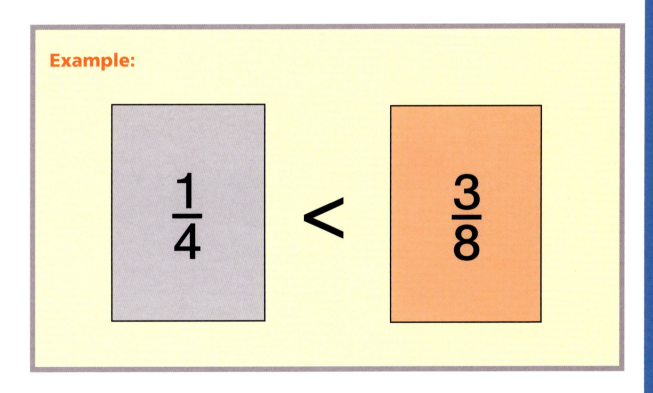

• You can use your completed table from lesson 3 to help you.

• If you cannot complete a number sentence, miss a turn.

• The winner is the first to complete six number sentences.

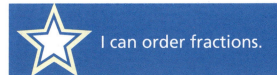
I can order fractions.

Sweet bar charts

You will need: squared paper

★ Jane sorted a box of sweets into colours and produced this frequency table.

Colour	red	green	brown	yellow	orange	pink	blue
Number of sweets	12	0	6	3	9	14	6

★ Copy the charts below onto squared paper.

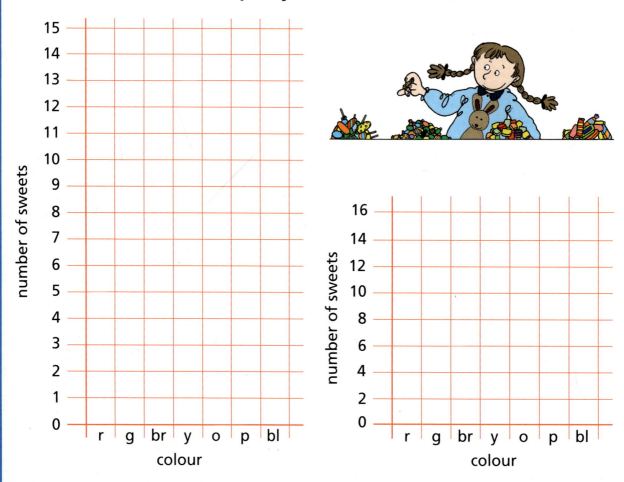

★ Make two bar charts showing the above data, one on each chart.

Challenge

★ Draw a chart marked in threes on squared paper.
★ Make a third bar chart showing the above data.

I can record frequency data on a bar chart.

Colourful cubes

> **You will need:**
> 100 coloured cubes
> squared paper

★ Work in groups of three or four.

❶ Sort the cubes into separate colours and record your results on a frequency table like the one below.

Colour	red	green	blue	yellow
Number of cubes				

❷ Show your results as a bar chart on squared paper. Before you start, think carefully about what scale you will use on the vertical axis and how you will label the axes.

❸ Think of four questions you can ask about the information on your bar chart. Write them down and ask them in the class discussion.

 I can record information in a frequency table and draw a bar chart.

Bird study

On a trip to the bird sanctuary, class 3B made a tally chart showing how many birds they saw. Here are their results:

Bird	Tally	Frequency
ducks	卌 卌 卌 II	
swans	IIII	
gulls	卌 卌 III	
geese	卌 卌 I	
terns	卌 卌 卌 卌	

★ Make a copy of the tally chart and complete the frequency column.
★ Construct a pictogram to show the data.

Think: What symbol will you use?
How many birds will each symbol represent?
Give your pictogram labels and titles.

❶ How many swans were seen?

❷ Which bird was seen most often?

❸ How many more ducks than swans were seen?

❹ How many pigeons were seen?

❺ What was the total number of birds seen and recorded?

I can construct a pictogram and read information from it.

Carroll clowns

You will need:
crazy clowns cards

★ Work with a partner.

★ Sort the clown cards according to two different criteria from the list below:
- hat/no hat
- happy/not happy
- bow tie/no bow tie
- curly hair/not curly hair

★ Draw a Carroll diagram like the one below to record your results.

★ Draw your own clown for a class Carroll diagram with the following labels:
- bow tie/no bow tie
- curly hair/not curly hair

I can organise data in a Carroll diagram.

Week 12 Lesson 4

Venn clowns

You will need:
crazy clowns cards

★ Work in groups of three or four.

★ Sort the clown cards according to two different criteria from the list below:
- hat
- happy
- bow tie
- curly hair

★ Record your results on a Venn diagram like the one below.

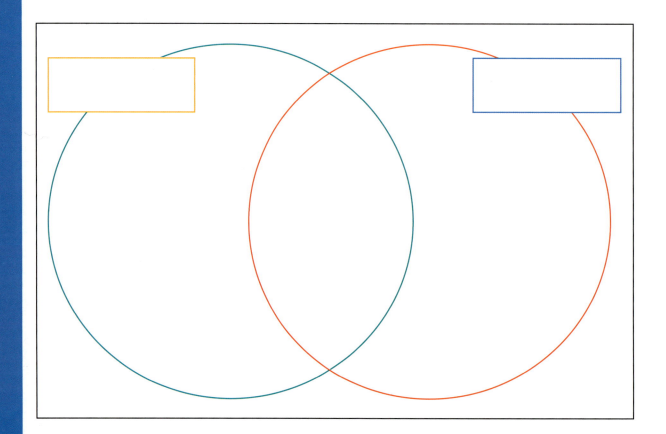

★ Draw your own clown for a class Venn diagram with the following labels:
- bow tie
- curly hair

I can organise data in a Venn diagram.